Cost Accounting Made Simple

Cost Accounting Explained
in 100 Pages or Less

Cost Accounting Made Simple

Cost Accounting Explained in 100 Pages or Less

Mike Piper

Dedication

For you, the reader, in the hope that accounting will be a useful tool throughout your career rather than a stumbling block or source of confusion.

Why is there a light bulb on the cover?

In cartoons and comics, a light bulb is often used to signify a moment of clarity or sudden under-standing—an "aha!" moment. My hope is that the books in the ...*in 100 Pages or Less* series can help readers achieve clarity and understanding of topics that are often considered complex and confusing— hence the light bulb.

Disclaimer

This book is not intended to be a substitute for personalized advice from a professional financial planner. Nothing contained within this text should be construed as financial advice. The publisher and author make no representation or warranty as to this book's adequacy or appropriateness for any purpose. Similarly, no representation or warranty is made as to the accuracy of the material in this book.

Purchasing this book does not create any client relationship or other advisory, fiduciary, or professional services relationship with the pub-lisher or with the author. *You alone* bear the *sole* responsibility of assessing the merits and risks associated with any financial decisions you make. And it should always be kept in mind that any investment can result in partial or complete loss.

Your Feedback Is Appreciated!

As the author of this book, I'm very interested to hear your thoughts. If you find the book helpful, please let me know! Alternatively, if you have any suggestions of ways to make the book better, I'm eager to hear that, too.

Finally, if you're dissatisfied with your purchase for any reason, let me know, and I'll be happy to provide you with a refund of the current list price of the book (limited to one refund per household).

You can reach me at: mike@simplesubjects.com.

Best Regards,
Mike Piper, CPA

Table of Contents

Part Three
Cost Assignment

Part Four
Budgeting and Variance Analysis

Why Read This Book?

Why would a person want to learn about cost accounting? What's the point? If you're currently asking yourself those questions, allow me to share a brief story about what can go wrong *without* proper cost accounting.

An acquaintance of mine worked for many years with a well known nonprofit organization. (I'm intentionally omitting the name, as my goal is not to embarrass anybody.) One of the ways this organization raised money was by holding three conferences each year in different parts of the country. The organization still struggled financially, as many nonprofits do. But if it weren't for the conferences bringing in money, things would have been much worse.

At least, that's what everybody thought.

Eventually, one of the organization's volunteers realized that there was an accounting error. Specifically, several costs that were the direct result of running these conferences (e.g., advertising the conferences, printing handouts, etc.) had been categorized simply as general costs of running the organization, rather than as costs of running the conferences.

Once all of the expenses were properly accounted for, it turned out that the conferences weren't particularly profitable. In fact, the organization was *losing* money on each conference it ran. The conferences weren't the thing keeping the organization afloat. They were part of the problem! And nobody even knew it—until someone arrived on the scene with a working knowledge of cost accounting.

The Goal of This Book

As with the other books in the *...in 100 Pages or Less* series, the goal of this book is not to teach you everything there is to know about the topic. That is, you will not be a cost accounting expert by the time you're finished reading. Rather, the goal is to provide a concise, easy to understand *introduction* to the topic, so that you're familiar and comfortable with the terminology and the basic concepts.

This book assumes that you have a basic knowledge of general accounting concepts such as the accounting equation and journal entries. If you could use a brief refresher, please see the appendix.

What We'll Be Covering

This book is organized into four sections.

Part 1 discusses what exactly cost accounting *is* and how it fits into the broader accounting picture.

Part 2 discusses the concept of fixed costs and variable costs, and how a business can use those concepts to estimate its profit (or loss) at various levels of sales volume.

In order to make good decisions, a business must know how much it costs to perform various activities (i.e., produce a given product or operate a given department). Part 3 of the book discusses cost assignment, which is the process that a business uses to collect such information.

Part 4 deals with business planning (in the form of budgeting) and variance analysis (i.e., the follow-up to the budgeting process, in which a business looks at how actual results compared to budgeted figures and whether there are any problems that need to be addressed).

PART ONE

Cost Accounting in the Big Picture

CHAPTER ONE

What is Cost Accounting?

Cost accounting is the process of measuring how much it costs a business to supply customers with the good or services that it sells.

Why is Cost Accounting Important?

Cost accounting is important because it provides business managers with information that is critical to running the business. For example, a business needs to know how much it costs to produce each of its products, otherwise it will make poor deci-sions about how much to charge for them.

Similarly, if a business has inaccurate information about how much it is spending to run one of its divisions, it may continue running that division for years, losing money the whole time without even realizing it. If the business had better information, it would realize that it needs to close down the division completely if it cannot improve profitability. The opposite problem can occur as well. For example, if costs are inappropriately allocated to a given product line, the business may incorrectly think that the product line is unprofitable (and choose to shut it down) when the division is actually earning a net profit for the company.

Cost accounting is also useful for finding the *source* of a problem. For example, if a business reaches all of its sales goals, but still has a less profitable month than it had anticipated, cost accounting provides the tools to figure out exactly *which* costs were higher than anticipated.

Managerial Focus

You may have noticed that in each of the examples above we are concerned with providing information to users *within* the business. Cost accounting is generally considered to be a part of *managerial* accounting, in which the primary goal is to provide the business's managers with the information they need to run the business effectively and profitably.

This is in contrast to financial accounting, which has primarily an external focus (i.e., producing financial statements for external users to be able to make decisions about whether or not to invest in the company, lend money to the company, etc.).

In financial accounting, it is critical that accountants follow GAAP (generally accepted accounting principles) so that external users can compare one company's financial statements to another company's—knowing that they were each made using the same set of rules and assumptions.

In managerial accounting it is the company that gets the final say in how it produces reports. That is, in managerial accounting, the company does not have to follow GAAP. Instead, the goal is simply to track and report information in whatever way will give the company the most useful information for decision-making.

A third difference between financial accounting and managerial accounting is that financial accounting is primarily about reporting on performance that has already occurred, whereas managerial accounting is more focused on making decisions about the future.

Cost accounting is, however, only a part of managerial accounting. Managerial accounting also includes several topics that we will not discuss in this book, such as capital budgeting and financial statement analysis.

Cost Accounting in Different Types of Businesses

While cost accounting is important for all types of businesses, *discussions* of cost accounting (and classes about cost accounting) tend to focus most heavily on manufacturing businesses rather than merchandising businesses or service-sector businesses. The reason for this focus on manufacturing businesses is simply that cost accounting is more complicated in such environments and therefore requires the most explanation.

For example, consider a business that manufactures watches. If the business has 1,000 finished watches in inventory at the end of a period, how much should it report as the cost of that inventory? That is, which expenses should be included in the cost for each watch? Labor? Materials? Electricity? Rent for the factory? And what if the business has not only 1,000 finished watches, but also 2,000 other watches in various stages of completion? How would it decide how much to report (in dollars) as the amount of inventory? Cost accounting provides the business with the tools to answer these questions.

In contrast, for merchandising businesses (which purchase and then sell already-finished goods), cost accounting is fairly straightforward. For example, if you run a clothing store, as long as you have good recordkeeping, it's easy to know exactly how much you paid for each pair of jeans in your inventory.

And cost accounting for service-sector businesses is simplified by the fact that such companies *have* no inventory. (At least, they have no inventory of goods to sell to customers. They do often have inventory of office supplies or other items.)

Chapter 1 Simple Summary

- Cost accounting is the process of measuring how much it costs a business to produce or supply goods/services.

- Cost accounting is considered to be a part of managerial accounting.

- In managerial accounting, the focus is on providing useful information to users *within* the company. (This is in contrast to financial accounting, which is focused on providing GAAP-compliant financial statements to *external* users.)

- Cost accounting is useful for all types of businesses. *Discussions* of cost accounting, however, tend to focus most heavily on manufacturing-sector businesses, simply because cost accounting is most complicated for those businesses.

CHAPTER TWO

The Flow of Costs in a Manufacturing Environment

In a retail/merchandising environment, inventory primarily consists of different products, all of which are ready to be sold. In a manufacturing environment, there are different *types* of inventory. At any given moment, there would be an inventory of completed units, an inventory of partially completed units, and an inventory of raw materials that have not yet been put into production at all.

As you might expect, there are separate accounts for each of these types of inventory. "Finished Goods Inventory" reflects the cost of all units that have been completed but not yet sold. "Work-in-Process Inventory" reflects the cost of units of production that are currently partially completed. And "Raw Materials Inventory" reflects the cost of raw materials that have not yet been used in production.

In other words, the flow of inventory looks like this:

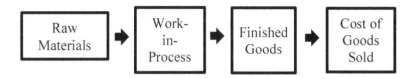

Following Product Costs

In cost accounting, there is an equation that we use to follow the flow of product costs through a business:

$$\text{Beginning inventory} + \text{Inputs} - \text{Outputs} = \text{Ending inventory}$$

This equation could be used, for example, to track a business's raw materials inventory levels.

EXAMPLE: Medical Manufacturing is a startup medical device maker. Medical had $5,000 of raw materials on hand at the beginning of the month. It purchased $70,000 of materials over the course of the month and placed $68,000 of materials into production over the course of the month. What is Medical's ending inventory of raw materials? To solve the question, we turn to our equation:

$$\text{Beginning inventory} + \text{Inputs} - \text{Outputs} = \text{Ending inventory}$$

In this case, purchases are our "inputs" (i.e., the amount that was added to raw materials inventory), and materials put into production are our "outputs" (i.e., the amount that was removed from raw materials inventory). So when we plug everything into our equation we get this:

$$\text{Beginning inventory} + \text{Purchases} - \text{Materials put into production} = \text{Ending inventory}$$

$5,000 + $70,000 - $68,000 = Ending inventory

Raw materials ending inventory = $7,000.

A key point here is that if we know any three of the amounts in the equation, we can calculate the fourth.

EXAMPLE: Medical Manufacturing had $10,000 of raw materials inventory on hand at the beginning of the month. It purchased $6,000 of raw materials over the course of the month and has $3,000 of raw materials inventory on hand at the end of the month. How much raw materials did Medical place into production during the month?

$$\text{Beginning inventory} + \text{Inputs} - \text{Outputs} = \text{Ending inventory}$$

$10,000 + $6,000 - put into production = $3,000

Conclusion: $13,000 of raw materials were put into production during the month.

Our flow of costs equation can be used not only for raw materials but also for other types of inventory. For instance, we can use it to calculate Work-in-Process inventory levels or cost of goods manufactured (CoGM).

"Cost of goods manufactured" refers to the cost of units that were completed during the period (regardless of whether those units were started in the period in question or a prior period). That is, it's the cost of units moved *out* of Work-in-Process and *into* Finished Goods.

EXAMPLE: Medical Manufacturing had $25,000 of Work-in-Process inventory at the beginning of the month. During the month, Medical incurred production costs of $60,000. Medical completed units worth $30,000 over the course of the month. What is Medical's month-end balance for Work-in-Process?

In this case, our inputs (i.e., the costs added to Work-in-Process inventory) are Medical's production costs, and our output (i.e., the costs removed from Work-in-Process inventory) is Medical's cost of goods manufactured for the month.

$$\text{Beginning inventory} + \text{Inputs} - \text{Outputs} = \text{Ending inventory}$$

$25,000 + $60,000 - $30,000 = Ending inventory

Ending inventory = $55,000

EXAMPLE: Medical Manufacturing had $15,000 of Work-in-Process inventory at the beginning of the month and $20,000 at the end of the month. During the month, Medical incurred production costs of $80,000. What is Medical's cost of goods manufactured for the month?

In this case, we're solving for "outputs," because CoGM is the amount moved *out* of Work-in-Process (and into Finished Goods) over the course of the month.

$$\text{Beginning inventory} + \text{Inputs} - \text{Outputs} = \text{Ending inventory}$$

$15,000 + $80,000 – Outputs = $20,000

Cost of goods manufactured = $75,000

We can also use the equation to calculate Finished Goods inventory levels or cost of goods sold for a given period.

As a reminder, "cost of goods sold" refers to the cost of units that were sold during the period. In other words, it's the cost of units moved *out* of Finished Goods during the period.

EXAMPLE: Medical Manufacturing had $10,000 of finished goods on hand at the beginning of the period. Medical's cost of goods manufactured was $81,000, and their cost of goods sold was $83,000. What is Medical's Finished Goods inventory at the end of the period?

Beginning inventory $+$ Inputs $-$ Outputs $=$ Ending inventory

Beginning inventory $+$ CoGM $-$ CoGS $=$ Ending inventory

$10,000 + $81,000 − $83,000 = Ending Inv.

Ending inventory = $8,000

A critical point to note here is that cost of goods manufactured is the cost of goods moved from Work-in-Process to Finished Goods. This is why it is the "output" when we're talking about Work-in-Process inventory and the "input" when we're talking about Finished Goods inventory.

Let's try one more example using Finished Goods inventory levels, CoGM, and CoGS.

EXAMPLE: Medical Manufacturing had $20,000 of Finished Goods on hand at the start of the period and $16,000 on hand at the end of the period. Medical's cost of goods manufactured for the period was $50,000. What was Medical's cost of goods sold?

Beginning inventory $+$ Inputs $-$ Outputs $=$ Ending inventory

$20,000 + $50,000 − CoGS = $16,000

Cost of goods sold = $54,000

Chapter 2 Simple Summary

- A manufacturing business will have separate inventory accounts for Raw Materials, Work-in-Process (i.e., units of production that are partially complete), and Finished Goods.

- Beginning inventory, plus inputs, minus outputs equals ending inventory. This concept is applicable to each type of inventory (i.e., raw materials, work-in-process, finished goods), and it can be used to calculate several different things, including cost of goods manufactured or cost of goods sold.

- Cost of goods manufactured (CoGM) is the cost of goods completed during the period. That is, it's the cost of goods moved *from* Work-in-Process *to* Finished Goods.

- Cost of goods sold (CoGS) refers to the cost of units that were sold during the period. That is, it's the cost that is moved *out* of Finished Goods during the period.

CHAPTER THREE

Control Accounts and Subsidiary Accounts

In accounting, sometimes we want very detailed information, and other times we want more of a summary. For example, with regard to accounts payable, the business itself clearly needs detailed information about exactly how much is owed to each of its creditors, so that it can pay each creditor on time. But an investor looking at the company's balance sheet probably doesn't care about how much is owed to one creditor rather than another. All the investor wants to know is the *total* amount that the company owes.

In accounting we use "control accounts" and "subsidiary accounts" so that we can provide detailed information when necessary and summary information when necessary. A control account reflects the sum of all of the balances of each of its subsidiary accounts. For example, a business would have a separate Accounts Payable account for each of its creditors. These would be the subsidiary accounts. And the sum of all of the balances in the Accounts Payable subsidiary accounts would be reflected as the balance in the Accounts Payable control account. (That is, the Accounts Payable control account would reflect *all* of the business's accounts payable.)

Control accounts are what ultimately show up in the company's major financial statements, while subsidiary accounts are more often used for various internal reports.

In cost accounting many of the accounts we've been discussing so far have subsidiary and control accounts. For example, the Raw Materials control account would often have several different subsidiary accounts, so that the business can track each of the different *types* of raw materials that it purchases. The Work-in-Process and Finished Goods inventory accounts would also typically have subsidiary accounts to track the different products that a company makes.

EXAMPLE: A contractor uses cash to purchase $7,000 of lumber and $3,000 of bricks. The transaction would be recorded with the following journal entry:

Raw Materials — Lumber	7,000	
Raw Materials — Bricks	3,000	
Cash		10,000

As a result of this entry, the two Raw Materials subsidiary accounts (lumber and bricks) would each reflect the necessary increase, and the Raw Materials control account would reflect the entire $10,000 increase.

Chapter 3 Simple Summary

- In accounting we use subsidiary accounts and control accounts so that we can show more detailed or less detailed information as necessary.

- Control accounts reflect all of the balances for that type of account. For example, the Raw Materials control account reflects all of the raw materials inventory that a business has on hand. Control accounts are what ultimately show up in the company's major financial statements.

- Subsidiary accounts provide more detailed information. For example, a manufacturing business would typically have separate Raw Materials subsidiary accounts for each of the different types of raw materials that it uses.

PART TWO

Planning with Fixed and Variable Costs

CHAPTER FOUR

Classifying Costs: Fixed vs. Variable

In cost accounting, we have several ways of categorizing the various costs that a business incurs. One such categorization involves determining how each cost behaves—specifically, whether it is a "fixed cost" or a "variable cost."

A fixed cost is one that does not vary as a function of production levels. Some common fixed costs would be: rent, insurance, property taxes, and pay for employees who are paid a flat salary.

A variable cost is one that *does* vary as a function of production levels. Common variable costs include materials used in production, hourly wages of employees who work in production, and costs of shipping finished goods to customers.[1]

---

[1] There are "mixed costs" as well (i.e., costs that have both a fixed component and a variable component), but for simplicity's sake our discussion will be limited to just fixed and variable costs.

EXAMPLE: Jason owns a small bakery, which specializes in making pies. He makes anywhere from 600-800 pies each month, depending on the season. (He finds that he has to make more pies per day during November and December than during the rest of the year, in order to accommodate greater demand during the holidays.)

Whether Jason makes 600 pies, 700 pies, or 800 pies in a given month, his rent does not change. His rent, therefore, is a fixed cost.

The total amount he spends on flour, butter, and fruit to fill the pies, however, *does* change when he makes more or fewer pies. That is, he'll spend more on ingredients in a given month if he makes 800 pies than if he makes 600 pies. His cost for ingredients is a variable cost.

The Relevant Range

The "relevant range" is the range of production across which our assumptions about fixed and variable costs hold true.

Consider Jason from our example above. What if he wants to dramatically ramp up production so that he's making 10,000 pies each month? In that case, the little kitchen in the storefront he rents won't be nearly large enough. He'll have to rent a larger space, and his rent will increase. His rent, which we have thus far considered to be a fixed cost, has now become a variable cost.

Point being, at some level of production (i.e., when we step outside the "relevant range"), even fixed costs will vary.

Outside of the relevant range, fixed costs often move in what is known as a "step function." That is, as the production level increases they *jump* upward rather than moving upward gradually (as a variable cost would). This would be the case for Jason's rent. When he moves to a larger kitchen, his rent would jump upward. From that point, however, his rent would stay level as the production level increased—until someday he has to move to yet another larger kitchen, at which point his rent would jump upward again.

Total vs. Per-Unit

The total amount Jason spends on butter changes depending on how many pies he makes. That's why butter is a variable cost for his business. However, the amount Jason spends on butter *per pie* does not change as a function of his output level.

In other words, variable costs vary *in total* based on output level, but are generally considered to be constant on a *per-unit* basis.

Conversely, fixed costs are fixed in total. But they vary on a per-unit basis. (That is, the more units the business produces, the lower the fixed cost per unit, because the fixed cost is spread out over more units.)

Chapter 4 Simple Summary

- A fixed cost is one that does not change as a function of output. That is, a business can increase or decrease its level of production without changing the total amount it spends on fixed costs.

- A variable cost is one that does change as a function of output. Materials used to produce a product would be a variable cost. (The more units produced, the more the business will have to spend on materials.)

- The relevant range is the range of output across which our assumptions about fixed costs and variable costs hold true. Outside of the relevant range, even fixed costs will vary.

- While fixed costs are fixed in total, they vary on a per-unit basis. That is, the more units produced, the lower the fixed cost per unit.

- While variable costs vary in total, they are assumed not to change on a per unit basis. That is, regardless of how many units are produced, the variable cost per unit is unchanged.

CHAPTER FIVE

Cost-Volume-Profit Analysis

One of the reasons we categorize costs as either fixed or variable is to be able to do a "cost-volume-profit analysis." Such an analysis lets a business know how many units it has to sell in order to earn a profit of a given size. Or, conversely, it calculates the amount of profit that will be earned if a given amount of units are produced and sold.

For simplicity's sake, in cost-volume-profit analysis, we assume that the number of units sold in a given period is the same as the number of units produced in that period.

The general equation that we use for cost-volume-profit analysis is as follows:

Profit = Sales – Variable costs – Fixed costs

EXAMPLE: Danielle owns a business that makes custom ("bespoke") suits. She charges $1,000 per suit. Her variable costs (primarily materials) are $200 per suit. Her fixed costs (rent and a handful of other smaller costs) are $3,000 per month.

If Danielle makes and sells 10 suits in a month, what will her monthly profit be?

Profit = Sales − Variable costs − Fixed costs

Profit = ($1,000 x 10) − ($200 x 10) − $3,000

Profit = $10,000 − $2,000 − $3,000

Profit = $5,000

Contribution Margin

When doing cost-volume-profit analysis, total variable costs and total revenue are the two things that change as volume changes. (Fixed costs don't change because they're fixed, assuming production stays within the relevant range.) The difference between a business's revenues and total variable costs is referred to as its "contribution margin." That is:

Contribution margin = Sales − Variable costs

EXAMPLE: Joe has a food truck from which he sells tacos. In the month of July, his fixed costs were $900, his total variable costs were $4,000, and his revenue was $10,000. Joe's contribution margin is $6,000 (i.e., his revenue minus his variable costs).

Contribution margin is particularly helpful when looked at on a per-unit basis. The per-unit contribution margin for a product is the difference between the product's selling price and the per-unit variable costs necessary to produce the product.

$$\text{Contribution margin per unit} = \text{Selling price} - \text{Variable cost per unit}$$

In other words, the per-unit contribution margin for a product is the amount that each unit of sales *contributes* toward the company's profits.

EXAMPLE: Joe sells his tacos for $5 each. His variable cost per taco is $2. His contribution margin per taco is $3 (i.e., $5 selling price minus $2 variable costs). Each taco sold *contributes* $3 toward covering his fixed costs. And after his fixed costs are covered for the period, each taco sold *contributes* $3 of profits.

Breakeven Analysis

One common use for cost-volume-profit analysis is to find a business's "breakeven point"—the number of units the business would have to sell in order to precisely break even in a given period.

EXAMPLE (continued): What is Joe's breakeven point? That is, how many tacos does he have to make and sell in order to break even in a given month?

Again, we know that Joe's fixed costs are $900 per month. And we know that his contribution margin is $3 per taco. (That is, each taco sold contributes $3 toward covering his fixed costs.) We can calculate his breakeven point by dividing his fixed costs by his contribution margin per unit.

$$\text{Breakeven point (in units)} = \frac{\text{Total fixed costs}}{\text{Contribution margin per unit}}$$

$$\text{Breakeven point (in units)} = \frac{\$900}{\$3 \text{ contribution margin per taco}}$$

Breakeven point = 300 tacos

Reaching a Target Operating Income

Cost-volume-profit analysis can also be used to calculate how many units of a product must be sold in order to achieve a given level of operating income (i.e., profit before interest and income tax expenses).

As we discussed previously, a company's contribution margin is equal its revenue minus variable costs. Another way to state that would be to say that a company's contribution margin is essentially its profit before considering fixed costs.

For example, if Joe wants to earn a profit of $5,100 in a given month with his taco truck business, and his fixed costs are $900 per month, how much contribution margin would be required? That is, how much contribution margin would be necessary to cover Joe's fixed costs and still provide the desired level of profit?

$$\begin{array}{c} \text{Required} \\ \text{contribution} \\ \text{margin} \end{array} = \begin{array}{c} \text{Target operating} \\ \text{income} \end{array} + \begin{array}{c} \text{Fixed} \\ \text{costs} \end{array}$$

Required contribution margin = $5,100 + $900

Required contribution margin = $6,000

If Joe's contribution margin per taco is $3, how many tacos will he have to sell in order to reach his desired level of operating income for the period?

$$\begin{array}{c} \text{Required} \\ \text{units sold} \end{array} = \frac{\text{Required contribution margin}}{\text{Contribution margin per unit}}$$

$$\begin{array}{c} \text{Required} \\ \text{units sold} \end{array} = \frac{\$6,000}{\$3 \text{ contribution margin per taco}}$$

Required units sold = 2,000 tacos

Contribution Margin Income Statement

In managerial accounting, businesses will often prepare an income statement (such as the one below) formatted in a way that highlights contribution margin.

Contribution Margin Income Statement		
	Total	Per Unit
Sales (2,000 units)	$10,000	$5
Variable costs	($4,000)	($2)
Contribution margin	$6,000	$3
Fixed costs	($900)	
Operating Income	$5,100	

With a traditional income statement, you begin with revenue, then subtract cost of goods sold (which includes both variable and fixed production costs) to arrive at gross profit. Then you subtract selling and administrative expenses (both fixed and variable) to arrive at operating income.

In contrast, with a contribution margin income statement, all variable costs (i.e., variable production costs as well as variable selling and administrative costs) are grouped together and subtracted from revenue to arrive at contribution margin. Then, all fixed costs (both production-related ones as well as selling and administrative ones) are grouped together and subtracted from contribution margin to arrive at operating income.

Chapter 5 Simple Summary

- Cost-volume-profit analysis lets a business know how many units it must sell in order to earn a profit of a given size. Or, conversely, it calculates the amount of profit that will be earned if a given amount of units are produced and sold.

- One common use for cost-volume-profit analysis is to find a business's "breakeven point"—the number of units the business would have to sell in order to precisely break even in a given period.

- Contribution margin refers to a business's revenue minus variable costs.

- Contribution margin per unit is equal to the per unit selling price minus the per unit variable costs. In other words, it's the amount that each unit of sales *contributes* toward the business's profits.

PART THREE

Cost Assignment

CHAPTER SIX

What is Cost Assignment?

One of the major goals of cost accounting is to collect information for the sake of answering questions like:

- Of the costs we incurred this month, how much of those costs were the result of making Product X?
- How much of the costs were a result of running Department Y?
- Which of the costs should be reflected on our balance sheet as inventory, and which costs should show up on the income statement as cost of goods sold or as other expenses?

In cost accounting, a "cost object" is anything for which we want a cost measurement (e.g., Product X or Department Y in the questions above).

"Cost assignment" is the process that allows us to answer these questions. That is, cost assignment is the process of assigning costs to cost objects (e.g., which of the costs we've incurred this month should be recorded as costs to produce Product X?).

In the next few chapters, we'll look at how a business decides which costs should be assigned to which cost objects.

Chapter 6 Simple Summary

- A cost object is anything (most often a product, but sometimes a department) for which we would like a cost measurement.

- Cost assignment is the process of assigning costs to cost objects.

CHAPTER SEVEN

A Hierarchy of Costs: Product and Period Costs

In cost accounting, costs are classified as either "product costs" or "period costs." Product costs are all the costs a business incurs to make or purchase the product(s) that it sells. Period costs are essentially all costs that aren't product costs. Whereas product costs are initially recorded as an asset (inventory) and later recorded as an expense (cost of goods sold) when the inventory is sold, period costs are recorded as an expense in the period in which they are incurred.

For a business that purchases the goods it sells, it's obvious which costs are product costs. For example, for a wine retailer, all of the money spent to purchase the wine it sells is a product cost.

For a business that manufactures the goods it sells, there are many types of product costs. For example, materials used in production, wages of production-line employees, depreciation of manufacturing equipment, repairs of manufacturing equipment, rent for a manufacturing plant, and several other costs would be product costs.

Typical period costs would include all of a firm's selling and administrative expenses (e.g., commissions of salespeople, advertising costs, salaries of office workers, and rent for office space).

A key point here is that certain costs could be product costs *or* period costs, depending on context. For example, wages would be a product cost if they are for the employees who work in a plant producing goods, but they would be period costs if they are for employees who perform selling or administrative functions.

Some costs can even be a combination of product cost and period cost and will have to be apportioned between the two categories. For example, imagine a small soap making business that rents a single location. Half of that location is used for production of the soap, while the other half is used for all of the business's selling and administrative activities. The business only receives a single rent bill each month, but half of that expense will be a product cost (to reflect the part that is spent on production), while the other half will be a period cost (to reflect the part that is spent on selling/administrative activities). And the same thing will be true for the firm's utility bill for that single location—it will be part product cost, part period cost.

Direct and Indirect Manufacturing Costs

For a company that manufactures the goods it sells, within the product cost category, costs are further broken down as follows:

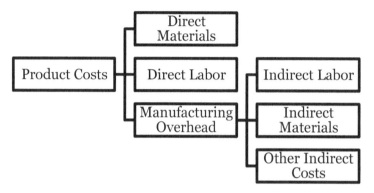

"Direct costs" are those that can be directly traced to a specific cost object. (As a reminder, a cost object is typically a product.) "Indirect costs" are those that cannot be directly traced to a single cost object. Because they cannot be traced directly to a specific cost object, indirect costs must instead be allocated to all of the products they are used to produce.[1]

---

[1] When we distinguish between direct costs and indirect costs, we're usually referring to product costs (i.e., determining whether a given product cost is a direct cost or an indirect cost). In some cases (especially when the cost object in question is a department rather than a product) period costs can also be classified as direct costs or indirect costs.

EXAMPLE: For a manufacturer of rock climbing gear, the cost of nylon for climbing ropes can be directly traced—it's obviously a cost of producing the ropes. It is a direct cost. Similarly, the aluminum used for carabiners is a direct cost because it can be directly traced as a cost of producing the carabiners.

But what about the electricity that's used to power the company's manufacturing facility? The facility produces several different products, including climbing ropes, carabiners, and climbing harnesses. As a result, the cost of electricity cannot be directly traced to a single product. It is an indirect cost. The firm will have to use some sort of system (which we'll discuss in Chapters 8-10) to *allocate* the cost of electricity among the various products that the electricity is used to produce.

To recap: Direct costs get directly traced. Indirect costs have to be allocated.

Direct Materials and Direct Labor

Direct manufacturing costs are further divided into two categories: "direct materials" and "direct labor." Direct materials include all materials that eventually become part of the finished product and that can be directly traced to a given product in an economical manner (e.g., the nylon used in a climbing rope). Direct labor includes the compensation for any labor that can be directly traced to a cost object. Of note: This includes not only wages/salary, but also other types of compensation such as health insurance, retirement benefits, and so on.

Indirect Manufacturing Costs (Manufacturing Overhead)

Indirect manufacturing costs—also referred to as manufacturing overhead costs—includes three types of costs: indirect materials, indirect labor, and other manufacturing overhead costs.

"Indirect materials" include all materials used in manufacturing which cannot be traced to specific cost objects in an economically feasible manner. Common examples of indirect materials would be cleaning supplies and lubricants for machinery. Screws, nuts, and bolts would often be included in indirect materials as well, because while it would be possible to directly trace them to specific products, it would not be cost-effective to do so. (That is, because screws, nuts, and bolts are so inexpensive, it doesn't often make sense to spend much time/money tracking them.)

"Indirect labor" includes costs for labor that is used in manufacturing but which cannot be directly traced to a specific cost object. Supervisors for a plant (who oversee production for all of the company's products) would be categorized as indirect labor. The cleaning crew that cleans the plant would also be indirect labor, as would the maintenance crew that handles repairs for the plant.

"Other manufacturing overhead costs"—also referred to as "other indirect manufacturing costs"—is just what it sounds like: any other costs of manufacturing that cannot be traced to a specific cost object. For example, if a manufacturing facility is used to produce multiple products, most costs applying to the entire facility (e.g., rent, insurance, utilities) would be in the other manufacturing overhead category.

Conversion Costs

"Conversion costs" refers to all the costs necessary to convert raw materials into a finished product. That is, all product costs other than direct materials are conversion costs. Said yet another way, conversion costs equals direct labor plus all indirect manufacturing costs (i.e., manufacturing overhead).

Chapter 7 Simple Summary

- Product costs are all the costs that a business incurs to produce or purchase the goods or services that it sells.

- Period costs are all costs that are not product costs. They are usually related to selling or administrative functions. Period costs are recorded as expenses in the period in which they are incurred.

- Direct costs are costs that can be directly traced to a specific cost object. Direct product costs include direct materials and direct labor.

- Indirect costs are costs that cannot be directly traced to specific cost objects. Indirect product costs (a.k.a., manufacturing overhead) are categorized as indirect materials, indirect labor, or other manufacturing overhead.

- Conversion costs are the costs necessary to convert raw materials into finished products. (Conversion cost = manufacturing overhead + direct labor.)

CHAPTER EIGHT

Job Order Costing

It is important for a business to be able to identify which product costs should be assigned to which units of production. Without this information, the business will not know how much it needs to charge for different products. It won't know which products are currently profitable. And it won't know what balance to report as inventory on the balance sheet as opposed to cost of goods sold on the income statement.

Broadly speaking, businesses use two types of costing systems for assigning costs to products or services:

1. Process costing (which we'll discuss more thoroughly in the next chapter), and
2. Job order costing.

Process costing is used when a business produces very large numbers of identical units of output (e.g., a Coke bottling plant).

Job order costing is used when a business provides goods or services that are made to order (i.e., specially made according to a customer's specifications). For example, job order costing would be used for an engineering company that designs bridges. Each bridge will be unique, specifically designed to satisfy an assortment of circumstance-specific requirements. Job order costing is very common for service businesses. For instance, law firms typically use job order costing to separately track the cost of each client/project.

It's worth noting that a job order costing system doesn't necessarily require that only one unit of production will be made for each job. For instance, imagine that you run a business creating costumes for movies. If you're hired to create twenty outfits of elven battle armor, those twenty outfits would be a single "job"—a single cost object.

The point is simply that process costing is suited to a business that churns out huge numbers of identical products (e.g., Apple producing many thousands of each model of iPhone), whereas job order costing makes more sense when smaller quantities of customized products are being made.[1]

---

[1] In the real world, many businesses use some sort of hybrid between the two. (Remember, the goal of managerial/cost accounting is to provide useful information to *internal* users, and a business can set up whatever cost accounting systems are most useful for their own decision-making.)

Job Order Cost Sheets

In a job order costing system, the document used to track the costs for a given job is known as a job order cost sheet. (These days, this is generally an electronic document.) The first section of a job order cost sheet typically includes several pieces of basic information about the job: the customer name, the job number, the date the job was begun, and a note describing the job. The next section of a job order cost sheet is where cost information would be entered. And costs for the job would be totaled at the end of the job order cost sheet.

Job Order Cost Sheet Example			
Job Number	501		
Customer	Mythic Production Studios		
Date Begun	9/1/2017		
Job Description	Elven battle armor		
Units	20		
Date	**Direct Materials**	**Direct Labor**	**Allocated Overhead**
9/1/2017	$200	$2,000	$100
9/8/2017	$300	$2,000	$100
9/15/2017		$2,000	$100
Subtotal:	$500	$6,000	$300
Total cost:			$6,800
Unit cost:			$340

Again, the direct materials and direct labor costs that appear here were directly *traced* to this job (i.e., we know from materials requisition forms and employee time sheets that these costs were clearly and directly related to this job). Conversely, the overhead costs were *allocated* to this job.

Allocating Overhead

In job order costing, overhead is allocated to jobs using a four-step process.

First, the business selects a "cost allocation base" that will be used as the basis for allocating manufacturing overhead costs. For example, the business might choose direct labor hours (or machine hours) as its cost allocation base, reasoning that if a job uses a lot of direct labor hours (or machine hours), the job was probably responsible for causing a lot of overhead costs as well.

Second, the business calculates the total budgeted manufacturing overhead costs for the period, as well as the total quantity of the cost allocation base that the business expects to use over the period (e.g., 5,000 direct labor hours).

Third, the business calculates an overhead allocation rate using those two budgeted amounts.

$$\text{Overhead allocation rate} = \frac{\text{Total budgeted overhead costs}}{\text{Total budgeted quantity of cost allocation base}}$$

Finally, overhead is applied throughout the period to each job using the *budgeted* allocation rate and the *actual* amount of the cost allocation base used for the job.

EXAMPLE: Cole Construction uses direct labor hours as its cost allocation base. Cole anticipates using 4,000 direct labor hours this month, and it has budgeted $8,000 as the total manufacturing overhead cost for the period. Over the course of the month, Cole uses a total of 150 direct labor hours producing Job #177. How much overhead will be allocated to Job #177?

First, Cole calculates its overhead allocation rate as follows:

$$\text{Overhead allocation rate} = \frac{\text{Total budgeted overhead costs}}{\text{Total budgeted quantity of cost allocation base}}$$

$$\text{Overhead allocation rate} = \frac{\$8,000}{4,000 \text{ direct labor hours}}$$

Overhead allocation rate = $2/direct labor hour.

Next, Cole applies overhead to each job as the job uses direct labor hours. In this case, Job #177 uses 150 direct labor hours, so Cole will allocate overhead as follows:

Applied overhead = $2/DL hour x 150 hours.

Applied overhead = $300.

At the end of the period, the total amount of overhead applied to all jobs will surely turn out to be more or less than the actual overhead costs incurred (because actual total overhead costs will vary from budgeted overhead costs, and because the actual amount of the cost allocation base used will vary from the budgeted amount). As a result, we have to do something to deal with under/over-applied overhead. The most common and simplest approach is simply to write the difference off to Cost of Goods Sold. (Some business, however, will choose to allocate it to specific jobs or allocate it among ending inventory accounts and Cost of Goods Sold.)

Journal Entries in a Job Order Cost System

What follows is a discussion of the journal entries that would be made as costs flow through a job order cost system. If you could use a refresher on the basics of journal entries, please read the appendix now. (Please note that the dollar amounts used in each of the following journal entries are simply made up, so don't spend any time trying to figure out where the specific numbers are coming from.)

When materials are purchased:
Raw Materials   5,000
    Accounts Payable   5,000

We debit Raw Materials (an asset account) to increase it, and we credit Accounts Payable (a liability account) to increase it. It's worth noting that an entry would probably be made at the same time to subsidiary accounts for Raw Materials (to show *which* type of Raw Materials was purchased) and Accounts Payable (to show *which* vendor we now owe money to).

When direct materials are used in production:

Work-in-Process	7,000	
Raw Materials		7,000

This journal entry records the decrease in Raw Materials inventory and moves the cost into Work-in-Process inventory.

An important point to note here is that an entry would be made at the same time to the Work-in-Process subsidiary ledger to show *which* subsidiary account would be increased (e.g., the one for Job #177). In a job order cost system, each job will typically have its own Work-in-Process subaccount.

When indirect materials are used in production:

Overhead	2,000	
Raw Materials		2,000

The Overhead account is basically a temporary holding place for indirect product costs. The

Overhead account doesn't actually show up on financial statements. Rather, we ultimately move the costs to other accounts when overhead gets applied to specific jobs.

The reason we put indirect costs in the Overhead account for the time being (rather than directly debiting Work-in-Process) is that indirect costs cannot be traced directly to a specific job, so we wouldn't know which Work-in-Process subsidiary account to debit. So we'll put it here for now, and later move the cost when we allocate overhead.

When payroll is recorded:
WIP (for direct labor)	15,000	
Overhead (for indirect labor)	4,000	
Wages Payable		19,000

When other overhead costs get recorded:
Overhead	6,000	
Accounts Payable		6,000

The credit in the above entry would be to cash if the business paid cash or to Accumulated Depreciation in the case of depreciation expense.

When overhead gets allocated to a specific job:
Work-in-Process	4,000	
Overhead		4,000

Again, an entry would be made at the same time to the Work-in-Process subsidiary ledger to show *which* job's subsidiary account would be increased.

When the product is finished:
Finished Goods	30,000	
Work-in-Process		30,000

This entry takes the cost of the job out of Work-in-Process and moves it into Finished Goods. Again, entries would also be made to subaccounts for Finished Goods and Work-in-Process to reflect *which* job was completed.

When the product is sold:
Cost of Goods Sold	30,000	
Finished Goods		30,000
Accounts Receivable	40,000	
Sales		40,000

This entry removes the cost of the job from Finished Goods and records it as Cost of Goods Sold. The second part of the entry records the revenue from the sale. (Note that the amounts are different, because the revenue from the job exceeds the cost of the job. That's a good thing.)

To clean up the difference between allocated overhead and actual overhead:
Overhead	7,000	
Cost of Goods Sold		7,000

As mentioned earlier in the chapter, overhead will usually turn out to have been under-applied or over-applied over the course of the period. That is, there will still usually be a balance in the Overhead account at the end of the period, which must be dealt with in some way. Most commonly, we write it off to Cost of Goods Sold, as in the above entry. (In the above entry, we're assuming that overhead was over-allocated and therefore requires a debit entry. If overhead had been under-allocated, however, the debit and credit in the above entry would be reversed.)

Chapter 8 Simple Summary

• In order to make good decisions about its products (e.g., how much to charge for them, which ones to continue producing and which ones to discontinue), a business must know how much it costs to make its products. Costing systems provide that information.

• Job order costing is used when a business makes unique, made-to-order products.

• In job order costing, each job is a cost object. That is, we want to track costs by job. As a result, each job has its own Work-in-Process subaccount.

CHAPTER NINE

Process Costing

In job order costing, each job is unique. Because each job is unique, the cost of a unit of
production will vary from one job to another. (To
revisit our costume producer example from last
chapter: The cost to produce one World War II
costume will be different from the cost to produce
one modern-era office worker costume.) As a
result, in job order costing we have to measure the
unique cost of each specific job. That's why each
job has its own Work-in-Process subaccount.

In contrast, process costing is used when
the business produces a large volume of identical
units. In such an environment, one unit of production costs the same as another unit of production,
so there's no need to track costs by job. In process
costing, we measure the *average* cost per unit.

Instead of accumulating costs at the job level, process costing accumulates costs at the *department* level. That is, in process costing, each
department has its own Work-in-Process subac-

count. We do this so that we can follow units (and costs) *through the production process*. We want to know, at any given point in time, how much Work-in-Process inventory we have in each department (i.e., each part of the manufacturing process) as well as how much inventory is currently finished and ready for sale.

EXAMPLE: Choice Chocolate Company is a chocolate bar manufacturer. In the production process, each bar of chocolate passes through three departments: mixing, molding, and packaging. With process costing, Choice Chocolate Company can say how many units of production—or how many dollars-worth of product—are currently in each part of the process (i.e., in each department) as well as how many units are currently complete and available for sale.

Equivalent Units

In process costing (and cost accounting in general) we often have to account for the amount of work that has been done so far on units that are only partially complete. For example, imagine a business that starts 100 units of production during a period and brings them 25% of the way toward completion. If we said that the business produced 100 units, we would be overstating the amount of work that was done—after all, they're not finished yet. On the other hand, if we said that the business didn't produce any units, we'd be understating the amount of work that was done (even though it's true that no units were actually finished). Instead, we say that the business produced 25 "equivalent units." In other words, the idea of equivalent units is to be able to express the amount of work done *in terms of fully complete units,* even when some of the units are not yet complete.

The Process Costing Process

So far we've been looking at units. What if we want to know dollar amounts? How many dollars worth of work-in-process inventory (or finished goods inventory) should Choice Chocolate report? To answer that question, process costing follows a five-step process:

1. Account for the flow of physical units,
2. Calculate the total equivalent units across which we will allocate production costs (i.e., the number of equivalent units in the department's Work-in-Process inventory at the end of the period, plus the number of units that were completed and transferred out of the department),
3. Calculate the total product costs to account for (i.e., the beginning costs in Work-in-Process inventory, plus costs added during the period),

4. Divide the total costs from step 3 by the equivalent units from step 2 to calculate the cost per equivalent unit,

5. Assign product costs to equivalent units (from step 2) using the cost per equivalent unit calculated in step 4.[1]

The above process would be applied separately for each department. There's a lot going on here, so lets walk through the process slowly, step by step. (To keep things simple in our examples, we'll just follow the process for a single department—Choice Chocolate Company's molding department.)

PROCESS COSTING STEP 1: First, we account for the flow of physical units.

EXAMPLE: At the beginning of the month, the molding department had 2,000 physical units in Work-in-Process inventory. During the month, 10,000 physical units were transferred *into* the molding department from the mixing department, and 9,000 physical units were transferred *out* to the packaging department. Using our equation from Chapter 2 (beginning inventory, plus inputs,

---

[1] Here we are using the simplest method of assigning costs to equivalent units: the "weighted average" method, in which each equivalent unit is given the same cost as other equivalent units. There is also a "first-in first-out" (FIFO) method in which different units can have different costs from each other.

minus outputs, equals ending inventory) we can calculate that the molding department has 3,000 physical units of in Work-in-Process inventory at month-end.

Process Costing, Step 1: Accounting for Physical Units

Beginning Work-in-Process	2,000
Transferred in	+10,000
Transferred out	−9,000
Ending Work-in-Process	3,000

PROCESS COSTING STEP 2: In the second step of process costing, we calculate the total equivalent units across which we will allocate production costs. That is, we find the sum of a) the units completed during the period and b) the equivalent units in ending Work-in-Process inventory.

Important note: When we talk about how complete a unit is, we're concerned with its completeness with respect to the work done *in that department*. As a result, units are always considered 100% complete when they leave the department in question, even if they will need further work in later departments.

EXAMPLE: As mentioned above, Choice Chocolate's molding department had 3,000 units in Work-in-Process at the end of the month, and 9,000 units were completed and transferred out of the department over the course of the month. The units in the molding department's ending Work-in-Process inventory were 30%-complete. Let's calculate the equivalent units across which we'll allocate production costs.

Process Costing Step 2
Calculating Equivalent Units

Ending Work-in-Process	3,000	
Percent complete	x 30%	
Ending WIP equivalent units		900
Units transferred out		+9,000
Total equivalent units		9,900

PROCESS COSTING STEP 3: In the third step of process costing, we calculate the total product costs (for the department in question) that need to be allocated to units. That is, we want to know the sum of a) the beginning costs in Work-in-Process inventory, plus b) the product costs incurred by the department over the period.

EXAMPLE: Choice Chocolate Company's molding department had a Work-in-Process balance of $3,800 at the beginning of the month. During the month, the department incurred product costs of $16,000. As such, $19,800 is the total cost that will have to be allocated to units of production.

PROCESS COSTING STEP 4: In the fourth step of process costing, we calculate the average cost per equivalent unit by dividing the total product costs from step #3 by the number of equivalent units calculated in step #2.

EXAMPLE: For this month, Choice Chocolate Company's molding department has a cost per equivalent unit of $2, calculated as:

$$\frac{\text{Total product costs}}{\text{Equivalent units}} = \frac{\$19,800}{9,900 \text{ units}} = \$2/\text{equivalent unit}$$

PROCESS COSTING STEP 5: In the fifth (final) step of process costing, we use the cost per equivalent unit calculated in step #4 to assign costs to specific units, so that we know what balance to reflect in Work-in-Process and what balance to indicate as the cost of goods completed and transferred to the next department (or transferred to Finished Goods inventory, if we're looking at the last department in the production process).

EXAMPLE: As mentioned above, Choice Chocolate Company's molding department has 900 equivalent units in ending Work-in-Process inventory, and it completed and transferred 9,000 units to the packaging department. Using the cost per equivalent unit ($2) that we calculated in the previous step, we can determine that the molding department will reflect an ending Work-in-Process balance of $1,800 (i.e., 900 equivalent units x $2 per equivalent unit). We can also determine that $18,000 of inventory was completed and transferred to the packaging department (i.e., 9,000 equivalent units x $2 per equivalent unit).

Important reminder: The above examples walk through the five steps of process costing for one department, but in actuality this entire process would be repeated for *each* department.[1]

Journal Entries in Process Costing

The journal entries to track the flow of costs through a process costing system are very similar to the journal entries used in a job order cost system. The primary difference is that we have separate Work-in-Process subaccounts for each *department*, whereas in job order costing we had separate Work-in-Process subaccounts for each *job*.

---

[1] Sometimes equivalent units are calculated separately for direct materials costs as opposed to conversion costs (i.e., direct labor and manufacturing overhead). This is done because direct materials costs are often added entirely (or mostly) at the beginning of the manufacturing process, whereas conversion costs are incurred more evenly *throughout* the process. For an example of how this would work, please see:
http://obliviousinvestor.com/separate-equivalent-units/

When materials are purchased:

Raw Materials   11,000
     Accounts Payable (or Cash)   11,000[1]

When raw materials are used by the mixing department:

Work-in-Process — Mixing   5,000
     Raw Materials   5,000

A similar entry would be made when the packaging department uses materials (i.e., wrappers), except it would be the packaging department's Work-in-Process subaccount that gets debited.

When payroll is recorded for direct labor:

Work-in-Process — Mixing   7,000
Work-in-Process — Molding   12,000
Work-in-Process — Packaging   4,000
     Wages Payable   23,000

Remember, a product cost is an indirect cost (i.e., manufacturing overhead) if we cannot trace it directly to a specific cost object. In job order costing, our cost objects were jobs. So we debited Overhead when we couldn't directly trace the cost to a specific job (and we therefore couldn't directly debit a specific Work-in-Process subaccount).

---

[1] As in the previous chapter, the amounts in these example journal entries are simply made up. So don't worry about where they're coming from.

In process costing, our cost objects are departments. It's usually obvious which department incurred a given cost, so there are fewer indirect costs in process costing. Still, if we can't tell which department incurred a given manufacturing cost, we debit the Overhead account.

When indirect materials are used:
Overhead	3,000	
Raw Materials		3,000

When indirect labor is recorded:
Overhead	28,000	
Wages Payable		28,000

When other overhead costs get recorded:
Overhead	14,000	
Cash/Accounts Payable		14,000

As a reminder, the Overhead account is just a temporary placeholder for indirect costs. It is eventually zeroed out as we allocate those costs to specific cost objects.

When overhead gets allocated/applied:
WIP — [appropriate department]	9,000	
Overhead		9,000

When units move from one dept. to next:
Work-in-Process — Molding	22,000	
Work-in-Process — Mixing		22,000

When units move from one dept. to next:

Work-in-Process — Packaging   41,000
       Work-in-Process — Molding   41,000

When product is finished:

Finished Goods   60,000
       Work-in-Process — Packaging   60,000

When product is sold:

Cost of Goods Sold   48,000
       Finished Goods   48,000
Accounts Receivable (or Cash)   75,000
       Sales   75,000

Chapter 9 Simple Summary

- Process costing is used when a business makes a very large quantity of identical units of a product.

- In process costing, costs are tracked by department, then allocated to units (as opposed to being tracked by job as in job order costing).

The steps of process costing (using the "weighted average" method) are as follows:

1. Account for the flow of physical units;
2. Calculate the number of equivalent units in the department's Work-in-Process inventory at the end of the period, plus the number of units that were completed and transferred out of the department;
3. Calculate the total production costs to account for (i.e., the beginning costs in Work-in-Process inventory, plus costs added during the period);
4. Divide the total costs from step 3 by the equivalent units from step 2 to calculate the cost per equivalent unit;
5. Assign product costs to equivalent units (from step 2) using the cost per equivalent unit calculated in step 4.

CHAPTER TEN

Activity-Based Costing

As we discussed in Chapter 7, indirect costs cannot be directly traced to specific cost objects/products. But we still want to know how much of a given indirect cost should be assigned (i.e., allocated) to each cost object.

And as we discussed in Chapter 8, a simple method for allocating indirect costs is to do it based on a single cost allocation base, such as direct labor hours. That is, the more direct labor hours a product requires, the more overhead gets allocated to that product.

The line of thinking behind "activity-based costing" is that there's an *assortment* of activities that cause indirect costs to be incurred, so it makes more sense to apply indirect costs to products based on the various cost-driving activities that are required to produce each product, rather than assigning indirect costs based solely on direct labor hours.

The first step of activity-based costing is to set up "cost pools" and identify their accompanying "cost drivers." A cost pool is a group of indirect costs that tend to increase when a certain activity happens. And a cost driver is the activity that *drives* costs in a certain cost pool.

EXAMPLE: In a manufacturing plant, machine maintenance costs might be grouped into a cost pool, with machine hours being designated as the cost driver for that cost pool. And labor costs for supervisors might be another cost pool, with direct labor hours being the cost driver for that cost pool. Quality control costs could be a third cost pool, with units of production being the cost driver.

In activity-based costing, after identifying cost pools and their cost drivers, you follow a 3-step process to allocate indirect costs to cost objects:

1. Total the costs in each cost pool.
2. Calculate an allocation rate for each cost pool, by dividing total costs for that cost pool by the applicable cost driver activity level for the period.
3. Allocate costs to cost objects by multiplying the rates calculated above by the cost driver activity levels for each cost object.

EXAMPLE: XYZ Manufacturing has decided to use three cost pools for its activity-based costing system: maintenance and utilities, supervisor costs, and quality control. The cost drivers will be machine hours, direct labor hours, and units produced, respectively.

The total costs in each pool and activity levels for the cost drivers are as follows:

Cost Pool	Total Costs in Pool	Cost Driver	Cost Driver Activity Level
Maintenance & Utilities	$30,000	machine hours	1,000 hours
Supervisor Costs	$40,000	direct labor hours	2,000 hours
Quality Control	$5,000	units produced	5,000 units

XYZ Manufacturing would then compute allocation rates for each cost pool as follows:

$$\text{Allocation rate} = \frac{\text{Total costs in pool}}{\text{Cost driver activity level}}$$

Maintenance & Utilities:
Allocation rate = $30,000 ÷ 1,000 hours
Allocation rate = $30/machine hour

Supervisor Costs:
Allocation rate = $40,000 ÷ 2,000 hours
Allocation rate = $20/direct labor hour

Quality Control:
Allocation rate = $5,000 ÷ 5,000 units
Allocation rate = $1/unit

Now that we have calculated allocation rates, we're ready to apply indirect costs to cost objects. Let's say that XYZ makes just two products: Product A and Product B. And the relevant cost driver information is as follows:

Product A:
- 800 machine hours
- 1,000 direct labor hours
- 1,000 units produced

Product B:
- 200 machine hours
- 1,000 direct labor hours
- 4,000 units produced

For Product A, indirect costs would be applied as follows:

800 machine hours	1,000 DL hours	1,000 units
x $30/machine hour	x $20/DL hour	x $1/unit
$24,000	$20,000	$1,000

Total indirect costs applied to Product A:
$24,000 + $20,000 + $1,000 = $45,000

And costs would be applied to Product B using a similar calculation:

200 machine hours	1,000 DL hours	4,000 units
x $30/machine hour	x $20/DL hour	x $1/unit
$6,000	$20,000	$4,000

Total indirect costs applied to Product B:
$6,000 + $20,000 + $4,000 = $30,000

A key point to note here is that in the above calculations we are only calculating the indirect costs for making the two products. If we wanted to know each product's *total* cost, we would also include the costs of direct materials and direct labor.

Another important point to note here is that, unlike job order costing and process costing, activity-based costing is not just about inventory valuation. Rather, it's about knowing all of the costs that are caused by a given cost object. So in some cases product costs *and* period costs will be allocated to cost objects (whereas in job order costing and process costing, only product costs are allocated to cost objects). For instance, if a given product line results in very high customer service costs, we want to allocate that cost to that product line, even though it's not a product cost (i.e., not a cost of producing the product).

The advantage of activity-based costing (relative to a system like job order costing, in which period costs are simply reflected on the income statement and in which a single allocation base is used to allocate overhead) is that it provides more detailed and accurate information about the cost of each activity. That additional information can help managers to make better decisions. Activity-based costing is, however, more costly to implement, given the additional work involved.

Chapter 10 Simple Summary

- Indirect costs cannot be directly traced to specific cost objects. As such, they must be *allocated* to cost objects.

- The line of thinking behind activity-based costing is that there are certain *activities* that drive up costs. If a product requires a lot of those cost-driving activities, more cost should be allocated to that product.

- A cost pool is a group of indirect costs that are increased by a certain activity.

- A cost driver is an activity that causes indirect costs to be incurred (i.e., it's the activity that drives up costs in a cost pool).

- In activity-based costing, we calculate an allocation rate for each cost pool by dividing the total costs in that cost pool by the activity level for the associated cost driver.

- We then apply costs to specific cost objects by multiplying the allocation rate calculated above by the cost driver activity level associated with a specific cost object.

PART FOUR

Budgeting and
Variance Analysis

CHAPTER ELEVEN

Budgeting

Budgeting is a critical part of running a business. A business that fails to budget properly may find that it is unable to meet customer deadlines as a result of having run out of a particular input needed for the production process. Or the business may find that it's unable to pay vendors on time—thereby incurring late fees—as a result of a cash flow shortage that could have been avoided with proper budgeting.

With regard to personal finance, people often think of budgeting as expense planning. But budgeting is not just about costs. While many people have reasonably predictable income due to a salary, a business must *estimate* its income for future periods.

Budgeting deals with non-financial information as well. For example, a business must estimate how many units it will need of each type of raw materials in order to satisfy its planned level of production for the period.

The Budgeting Process

A typical budgeting process for a business would look something like this:

- Prepare the sales budget,
- Prepare the production budget,
- Prepare the direct materials, direct labor, and manufacturing overhead budgets,
- Prepare the cost of goods sold budget,
- Prepare the selling & administrative expense budget,
- Prepare budgeted financial statements (i.e., income statement, cash flow statement, balance sheet, and statement of retained earnings),
- Repeat as necessary until the business has a workable plan for the period.[1]

Essentially, the idea is to start with the sales budget and to work backward from there to see what will be necessary in order to have sufficient product on hand to satisfy the projected level of sales. (That is, how many units will have to be produced? And what costs will be incurred to produce those units?) Then, once we have infor-

---

[1] The budgeted income statement, together with all of the budgets leading up to the budgeted income statement, are collectively known as the business's "operating budget." The other budgeted financial statements are collectively known as the "financial budget."

mation about budgeted revenues and expenses, we can prepare budgeted financial statements.

A key point to understand here is that it's not the accounting department that does the budgeting. Or rather, it's not *just* the accounting department. For instance, a sales budget is prepared by sales managers (or by the accounting department with input from sales managers). And the same thing will be true with all of the other budgets—they require participation by the other affected departments.

The Sales Budget

As mentioned above, the budgeting process begins with a budget that forecasts sales for the period.

Example Sales Budget	
Projected sales (units)	50,000
Price per unit	x $70
Projected net sales	$3,500,000

It's worth noting that we're making two simplifications here.

First, many businesses choose to prepare a few different versions of the sales budget: one using optimistic assumptions, one using neutral assumptions, and one using pessimistic assumptions. If the sales budget is prepared in such a way, each of the other budgets will have to include those same versions as well, because the actions necessary to meet one level of sales are different from those necessary to meet a different level of sales. To keep our discussion simple, however, we're going to assume in the rest of this chapter that only one sales projection is made.

Second, a sales budget (and following budgets) will generally be more complex than our example here, as it usually has to be broken down to show projected sales for multiple products. It may also be broken down to show projected sales during various sub-periods (e.g., quarters or months within the year).

The Production Budget

Once the business has a projection for expected sales over the coming period, it can prepare a production budget. The production budget asks how many units have to be made in order to satisfy the projected level of sales as well as provide the desired level of end-of-period inventory. (A key point: This budget only deals with units, not dollars.)

Here we're basically just using the same equation that we used in Chapter 2: beginning inventory + inputs − outputs = ending inventory. In this case, however, we are solving for "inputs" (i.e., the necessary level of production, given all the other pieces of the equation).

Example Production Budget

Projected sales	50,000
Desired ending finished goods inv.	+20,000
Total required units	70,000
Beginning finished goods inventory	−15,000
Required production	55,000

Direct Materials, Direct Labor, and Overhead Budgets

Once the business knows how many units it will have to produce, it can budget for the necessary expenses. (These budgets deal with units *and* costs.)

The direct materials budget asks how many units of each type of raw materials must be purchased in order to satisfy the projected level of production as well as provide the desired level of end-of-period materials inventory. For example, if our business needs to produce 55,000 units of output over the period and each unit of output requires two units of material 1 and three units of material 2, the direct materials budget could look as follows:

Example Direct Materials Budget

	Material 1	Material 2
Required for production	110,000	165,000
Desired ending inv.	+40,000	+70,000
Total required units	150,000	235,000
Beginning inventory	−35,000	−65,000
Required purchases	115,000	170,000
Price per unit	x $2.00	x $5.00
Required purchases ($)	$230,000	$850,000

The direct labor budget uses the budgeted level of production together with information about a) the hours of direct labor necessary to produce each unit and b) the firm's expected wage rate per direct labor hour to calculate the budgeted direct labor cost.

Example Direct Labor Budget

Required production	55,000
Hours required per unit	x 0.5
Total budgeted DL hours	27,500
Direct labor wage rate	$18
Budgeted direct labor cost	$495,000

The company's indirect manufacturing costs (i.e., manufacturing overhead) need to be budgeted as well. The manufacturing overhead budget projects the company's fixed overhead costs such as rent and insurance for the manufacturing plant, salaried indirect labor (e.g., manufacturing supervisors who are paid the same amount regardless of activity level at the plant), and depreciation. It also uses the planned production level to budget variable overhead costs such as indirect materials, hourly indirect labor, and utilities.

Example Manufacturing Overhead Budget

Budgeted fixed costs

Rent for plant	8,000	
Insurance on plant	1,500	
Salaried indirect labor	8,500	
Depreciation	+16,000	
		$34,000

Budgeted variable costs

Indirect materials	11,000	
Hourly indirect labor	14,000	
Utilities	+6,000	
		$31,000
Total manufacturing overhead		$65,000

Cost of Goods Sold Budget

Now that the business has a production budget, direct materials budget, direct labor budget, and manufacturing overhead budget, it has all the information necessary to prepare a cost of goods sold budget. The first step is to calculate direct materials used in production, using our "beginning inventory + inputs − outputs = ending inventory" equation. (In this case, we're solving for outputs.)

Example Cost of Goods Sold Budget

Beginning DM inventory	$395,000
DM purchases	$1,080,000
DM ending inventory	−$430,000
DM used in production	$1,045,000

After we know the amount of direct materials used, we combine that with the direct labor cost and manufacturing overhead cost to calculate our cost of manufacturing for the period.

Cost of Goods Sold Budget (Continued)

Direct materials	$1,045,000
Direct labor	$495,000
Manufacturing overhead	+ $65,000
Total manufacturing cost	$1,605,000

Once we know the total manufacturing cost for the period, we can use that information as well as information about work-in-process inventory levels to calculate cost of goods manufactured. (As you may remember from Chapter 2, cost of goods manufactured refers to the cost of units that were completed during the period. That is, it's the cost of units moved *out* of Work-in-Process and *into* Finished Goods.) We are again using the same "beginning + inputs − outputs = ending" equation and solving for "output."

Cost of Goods Sold Budget (Continued)	
Beginning work-in-process	$320,000
Total manufacturing cost	+$1,605,000
Ending work-in-process	−$290,000
Cost of goods manufactured	$1,635,000

Finally, we can use our cost of goods manufactured total, together with information about finished goods inventory levels, to calculate cost of goods sold. (As discussed in Chapter 2, cost of goods sold refers to the cost of units that were sold during the period. In other words, it's the cost of units moved *out* of Finished Goods during the period.) Once again, we're using the same "beginning + inputs – outputs = ending" equation and solving for "output."

Cost of Goods Sold Budget (Continued)	
Beginning finished goods inv.	$400,000
Cost of goods manufactured	+$1,635,000
Cost of goods available for sale	$2,035,000
Ending finished goods inv.	−$450,000
Cost of goods sold	$1,585,000

Selling and Administrative Expense Budget

The business must also budget for the expenses that are not costs of producing/purchasing prod-

uct that will be sold. That is, to revisit the terminology from Chapter 7, this is a budget for the
business's *period* costs as opposed to *product*
costs.

Example Selling and Administrative Expense Budget

Office rent	2,300
Office utility expense	400
Office supplies	150
Salaries (non-production employees)	60,000
Commissions	150,000
Advertising	20,000
Insurance	+15,000
Total selling and administrative expenses	$247,850

Budgeted Financial Statements

At this point, the business finally has enough
information to prepare budgeted financial statements (sometimes referred to as "pro forma"
financial statements). These financial statements
are very much like regular financial statements,
aside from the fact that they are prepared *prior* to
the period in question, using budgeted information, rather than being prepared after the close
of a period, using information about the transac-
tions that actually occurred.

Of particular importance is the budgeted cash flow statement. The business must make sure it has sufficient cash on hand to be able to satisfy all of its planned cash outflows. If it looks like the currently projected cash inflows will be insufficient, the business will have to come up with a plan to raise additional cash (e.g., borrowing) or cut expenses.

This raises a critical point about the budgeting process: we may realize at some point that we have to go back to an earlier step in the process to adjust our plans. For example, while preparing the budgeted cash flow statement we might find that we need to borrow a significant amount of money—perhaps more than the business wants to borrow or *can* borrow—in order to satisfy projected cash outflows. In such a case, we have to go back to earlier steps to see how we can reduce the cash needed. Maybe we can cut expenses in certain places. If we do adjust our planned expenses, the relevant budget (and all other budgets using that information) must be updated to reflect the change. The budgeting process may require several iterations before a complete, workable plan is developed.

Chapter 11 Simple Summary

- The budgeting process starts with the sales budget, then works backwards from there to determine what activities and expenses will be necessary to satisfy that level of sales.

- After revenue and expense amounts are budgeted, the company can prepare budgeted financial statements.

- A major goal of the budgeting process is to make sure there are no shortfalls. For example, how many units of inventory will we need to produce in order to have enough on hand to satisfy sales? How many units of materials will we have to purchase in order to produce the required number of units? Will we have enough cash to satisfy our expenses and other liabilities, or do we have to plan to cut costs or raise cash in some other way (e.g., borrowing)?

- The budgeting process often requires multiple iterations in order to develop a workable plan.

CHAPTER TWELVE

Variance Analysis

It's a fact of life that things never proceed exactly according to plan. Sales may be higher or lower than budgeted. Expenses may be higher or lower than budgeted. Some customers may be unexpectedly late in paying their bills.

Variance analysis is the process of comparing actual results to budgeted figures, and seeing what we can learn from the differences (i.e., the "variances"). Variance analysis is useful as a tool for spotting small problems before they become big problems. It's also useful as a tool for spotting something that's working better than expected.

Standard Costs

In cost accounting, the budgeted amount for something is often referred to as a "standard." The "standard cost" per unit is the budgeted cost per unit (i.e., the budgeted cost of direct materials, direct labor, and manufacturing overhead). That is:

$$\begin{matrix} \text{Standard} \\ \text{cost} \end{matrix} = \begin{matrix} \text{Budgeted} \\ \text{DM cost} \end{matrix} + \begin{matrix} \text{Budgeted} \\ \text{DL cost} \end{matrix} + \begin{matrix} \text{Budgeted} \\ \text{OH cost} \end{matrix}$$

The difference between the standard cost and actual cost incurred is referred to as a "variance." We can calculate separate variances for direct materials, direct labor, and manufacturing overhead. The sum of those three variances is our total manufacturing variance. That is:

$$\begin{matrix} \text{Total} \\ \text{variance} \end{matrix} = \begin{matrix} \text{DM} \\ \text{variance} \end{matrix} + \begin{matrix} \text{DL} \\ \text{variance} \end{matrix} + \begin{matrix} \text{OH} \\ \text{variance} \end{matrix}$$

Variances are described as either "favorable" or "unfavorable," depending on how they impact operating income. When a cost turns out to be higher than expected, the variance is said to be unfavorable. And when a cost turns out to be lower than expected, the variance is said to be favorable.

Direct Materials Standard Costs

The "standard quantity of direct materials" is the budgeted quantity of direct materials necessary to make a unit of output. Of note, this includes any direct materials that are likely to get wasted in production as scrap/spoilage.

The "standard price of direct materials" is the budgeted price per unit of direct materials input.

Direct Materials Variances

To calculate direct materials variance, we ask, "for this level of production, how much would I *expect* to have spent on direct materials, and how much did I *actually* spend?"

Direct materials variance is broken down into price variance and quantity variance. Price variance asks whether we spent more or less per unit of direct materials input than we expected to spend. And quantity variance asks whether we used more or fewer units of direct materials input than we would have expected to use, given our level of output.[1]

We calculate direct materials price variance and quantity variance as follows:

$$\begin{matrix} \text{DM price} \\ \text{variance} \end{matrix} = \left(\begin{matrix} \text{Standard} \\ \text{price} \end{matrix} - \begin{matrix} \text{Actual} \\ \text{price} \end{matrix} \right) \times \begin{matrix} \text{Actual} \\ \text{quantity} \end{matrix}$$

$$\begin{matrix} \text{DM} \\ \text{quantity} \\ \text{variance} \end{matrix} = \left(\begin{matrix} \text{Standard} \\ \text{quantity} \end{matrix} - \begin{matrix} \text{Actual} \\ \text{quantity} \end{matrix} \right) \times \begin{matrix} \text{Standard} \\ \text{price} \end{matrix}$$

---

[1] Direct materials quantity variance is sometimes referred to as direct materials usage variance.

EXAMPLE: Jane's is a small clothing manufacturer that makes blue jeans. Regarding direct materials, Jane's standard quantity is 1.5 yards of denim per pair, with a standard price of $20 per yard. In other words, with respect to direct materials, the standard cost is $30 per pair of jeans. Jane's produced 500 pairs of jeans this period, using 900 yards of denim at a cost of $21 per yard. What is Jane's direct materials variance, and how is it broken down between price variance and quantity variance?

Jane's total direct materials cost was $18,900 (i.e., 900 yards x $21 per yard) when it was expected to be $15,000 (i.e., $30 standard cost x 500 pairs of jeans). So the total direct materials variance is $3,900, unfavorable.

As mentioned above, to calculate direct materials price variance, we find the difference between the standard price and the actual price, and we multiply that difference by the actual quantity used. In this case, the difference is $1 per yard ($20 standard, minus $21 actual price). And the actual quantity used was 900 yards. So the direct materials price variance is $900, and it is unfavorable because the actual price was greater than the standard price.

To calculate direct materials quantity variance, we find the difference between the standard quantity and the actual quantity, and we multiply that difference by the standard price. In this case the standard quantity would have been 750 yards (1.5 yards standard, times 500 pairs of jeans). And the actual quantity was 900 yards. So we have a difference of 150 yards. We multiply that difference by the standard price of $20 per yard, and we get a direct materials quantity variance of $3,000. The variance is unfavorable because the actual quantity used was greater than the standard quantity.

It's always good to quickly check to make sure that your DM price variance and DM quantity variance add up to the figure calculated for your total DM variance. In this case, our $900 unfavorable DM price variance and $3,000 unfavorable DM quantity variance do add up to the $3,900 unfavorable total DM variance we calculated earlier, so everything looks good.

Direct Labor Standard Costs

"Standard hours of direct labor" refers to the budgeted direct labor hours necessary to produce one unit of output. Of note, this includes breaks, setup times, and any other periods of non-work for which laborers must still be compensated.

The "standard rate of direct labor" (or "standard price of direct labor") is the budgeted cost of an hour of direct labor.

Direct Labor Variances

To calculate direct labor variance, we ask "for this level of production, how much would I expect to have spent on direct labor, and how much did I actually spend?" Like direct materials variance, direct labor variance is broken down into price variance and quantity variance.[1]

We calculate direct labor price variance and quantity variance as follows. (Not coincidentally, these equations look very much like the equations to calculate DM variances. We're doing the same calculations, just with labor-related inputs.)

$$\text{DL price variance} = \left(\text{Standard rate} - \text{Actual rate} \right) \times \text{Actual hours}$$

$$\text{DL quantity variance} = \left(\text{Standard hours} - \text{Actual hours} \right) \times \text{Standard rate}$$

EXAMPLE: Jane's standard hours of direct labor is 0.5 hours per pair of jeans, at a standard rate of $15 per hour. So Jane's standard direct labor cost per pair of jeans is $7.50. Jane's produced 500 pairs of jeans this period, using 240 hours of direct labor at a cost of $18 per hour. What is Jane's direct labor variance, and how is it broken down between price variance and quantity variance?

---

[1] Direct labor quantity variance is sometimes referred to as direct labor efficiency variance.

Jane's total direct labor cost was $4,320 (240 hours x $18 per hour) when it was expected to be $3,750 (i.e., $7.50 standard cost x 500 pairs of jeans). So the total direct labor variance is $570, and it is unfavorable because the actual costs exceeded standard costs.

To calculate direct labor price variance, we find the difference between the standard hourly rate and the actual hourly rate, and we multiply that difference by the actual quantity of direct labor hours used. In this case, the difference is $3 per hour ($15 standard, minus $18 actual price). And the actual quantity used was 240 hours. So the direct labor price variance is $720, and it is unfavorable because the actual hourly rate was greater than the standard hourly rate.

To calculate direct labor quantity variance, we find the difference between the standard quantity of hours and the actual quantity of hours, and we multiply that difference by the standard rate. In this case the standard quantity would have been 250 hours (0.5 hour standard, times 500 pairs of jeans). And the actual quantity was 240 hours. So we have a difference of 10 hours. We multiply that difference by the standard rate of $15 per hour, and we get a direct labor quantity variance of $150. The variance is favorable because the actual quantity used was less than the standard quantity.

Again, it's a good idea to check that our price variance and quantity variance add up to the total variance that we calculated earlier. In this case, we have an unfavorable price variance of $720 and a favorable quantity variance of $150. When netted against each other, the result is a total direct labor variance of $570, unfavorable, which matches our earlier calculation.

Manufacturing Overhead Variances

Manufacturing overhead variance is often broken down into fixed overhead variance and variable overhead variance.

Fixed overhead variance is easy to calculate. We simply compare the actual fixed overhead costs incurred over the period to the fixed overhead costs that were budgeted for the period.[1]

Fixed overhead variance	=	Budgeted fixed overhead	−	Actual fixed overhead

---

[1] There is also production volume variance, which is a function of how the number of units actually produced in a period compares to the number of units budgeted for production. If actual production exceeds budgeted production, this variance is said to be favorable, because you got more "bang for the buck" out of your overhead costs. Conversely, if actual production is lower than budgeted production, production volume variance is unfavorable.

EXAMPLE: Jane's budgeted a total of $1,700 in fixed overhead costs for the period. The business's actual fixed overhead costs came to $1,600 for the period. Jane's fixed overhead variance is $100, favorable.

Calculating variable overhead variance is somewhat more involved. Like direct labor variance and direct materials variance, variable overhead variance is broken down into price variance and quantity variance. In the case of overhead, however, we refer to them as "spending variance" and "efficiency variance."

To calculate these variances, we need to know what cost driver the business uses to allocate its overhead costs (e.g., machine hours or direct labor hours). We also need to know the budgeted (i.e., "standard") amount of the cost driver in question per unit of output (e.g., 3 machine hours or direct labor hours per unit of output). And we need to know the budgeted variable overhead cost per unit of that cost driver (e.g., $10 of budgeted variable manufacturing overhead per machine hour). Once we have all of that information, we can calculate variable overhead (VOH) spending variance and variable overhead efficiency variance as follows[1]:

---

[1] Again, it is not a coincidence that these equations look very much like the equations for DM price and quantity variances (or DL price and quantity variances). We're basically doing the same exact math.

$$\begin{array}{c}\text{VOH} \\ \text{spending} \\ \text{variance}\end{array} = \left(\begin{array}{c}\text{Budgeted} \\ \text{VOH cost} \\ \text{per unit of} \\ \text{cost driver}\end{array} - \begin{array}{c}\text{Actual} \\ \text{VOH cost} \\ \text{per unit of} \\ \text{cost driver}\end{array}\right) \text{x} \begin{array}{c}\text{Actual} \\ \text{quantity of} \\ \text{cost driver} \\ \text{used}\end{array}$$

$$\begin{array}{c}\text{VOH} \\ \text{efficiency} \\ \text{variance}\end{array} = \left(\begin{array}{c}\text{Budgeted} \\ \text{quantity of} \\ \text{cost driver} \\ \text{given actual} \\ \text{output level}\end{array} - \begin{array}{c}\text{Actual} \\ \text{quantity of} \\ \text{cost driver} \\ \text{used}\end{array}\right) \text{x} \begin{array}{c}\text{Budgeted} \\ \text{VOH cost} \\ \text{per unit of} \\ \text{cost driver}\end{array}$$

EXAMPLE: Jane's allocates overhead based on direct labor hours (i.e., direct labor hours is the cost driver for overhead). As discussed above, Jane's standard hours of direct labor is 0.5 hours per pair of jeans. Jane's budgets $2 of variable overhead per direct labor hour. Therefore, with respect to variable manufacturing overhead, Jane's standard cost per pair of jeans is $1.

Jane's produced 500 pairs of jeans this period, using 240 direct labor hours. Total variable overhead was $408. What is Jane's total variable overhead variance, and how is that broken down between variable overhead spending variance and variable overhead efficiency variance?

Given a standard cost of $1 per pair of jeans, total variable manufacturing overhead of $500 would have been expected for the 500 pairs of jeans produced. As such, total variable overhead variance is $92, and it is favorable because the actual cost was less than the standard cost.

To calculate variable manufacturing overhead spending variance, we find the difference between the budgeted variable overhead cost per unit of the cost driver and the actual variable overhead cost per unit of the cost driver. Then we multiply that difference by the actual quantity of the cost driver used. As mentioned above, the budgeted variable overhead rate was $2 per direct labor hour. As it turned out, actual variable overhead per direct labor hour was $1.70 ($408 ÷ 240 hours). So we have a difference of $0.30 per hour, which we will multiply by the actual direct labor hours used (240) to arrive at a variable overhead spending variance of $72. This variance is favorable because the actual overhead per hour was less than the standard overhead per hour.

To calculate variable overhead efficiency variance, we find the difference between the standard quantity of the cost driver and the actual quantity of the cost driver, and we multiply that difference by the budgeted variable overhead cost per unit of the cost driver. In this case the standard quantity would have been 250 hours (0.5 hour standard, times 500 pairs of jeans). And the actual quantity was 240 hours. So we have a difference of 10 hours. We multiply that difference by the budgeted variable overhead cost of $2 per hour, and we get a variable overhead efficiency variance of $20. The variance is favorable because the actual amount of the cost driver used was less than the standard amount.

Again, it's a good idea to check that our spending variance and efficiency variance add up to the total variance that we calculated earlier. In this case, we have a favorable spending variance of $72 and a favorable efficiency variance of $20. When added together, the result is a total variable overhead variance of $92, favorable, which matches our earlier calculation.

Variances: The Big Picture

In short, total manufacturing variance can be broken down as follows:

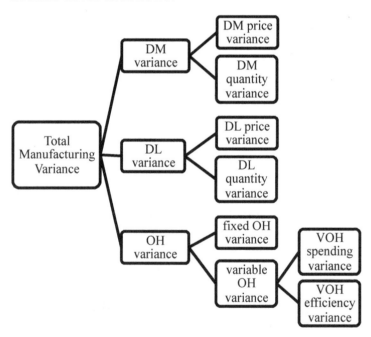

Investigating Variances

Despite their names, a favorable variance isn't *necessarily* a good thing, and an unfavorable variance isn't *necessarily* a bad thing.

Consider, for instance, a favorable direct materials price variance. Such a variance *does* increase net income for this period. But it could still be a negative thing overall, if it's due to a purchasing manager buying low-quality materials that will lead to poor product quality, low customer satisfaction, and long-term problems for the business.

Or consider a period in which a business's sales are much higher than expected. The business may need its production employees to work overtime in order to satisfy the demand. Those overtime hours will probably result in an unfavorable direct labor price variance, but that variance isn't the result of something going wrong. It's the result of something going *right* (higher than expected sales). If the business expects to maintain the higher level of sales, it should probably hire more workers. If the business thinks that the burst in sales is a one-time event, simply paying overtime for a short period may be preferable.

The overall point is simply that big variances (whether favorable or unfavorable) need *investigation*. We have to figure out the cause for the variance and whether or not it's something that demands action.

Chapter 12 Simple Summary

- Variance analysis is the natural follow-up to the budgeting process. It provides information for preparing a more accurate budget for the following period. And it helps identify potential problems.

- A favorable variance increases net income, and an unfavorable variance decreases net income.

- Despite the above point, a favorable variance isn't *necessarily* a good thing, and an unfavorable variance isn't *necessarily* a problem. What we can safely say about variances is that, if they are significant, they require investigation so that the business can determine a) the cause of the variance and b) whether or not action is required to address the cause of the variance.

CONCLUSION

Cost Accounting is Critical for Decision-Making

Cost accounting is the process of measuring how much it costs a business to provide goods or services to its customers. Cost accounting is considered to be a part of managerial accounting. In managerial accounting, the primary focus is on providing useful information to users *within* the company. (This is in contrast to financial accounting, which is focused on providing information—in the form of GAAP-compliant financial statements—to external users.)

A significant part of cost accounting is the act of classifying costs in various ways to assist in various types of decision-making.

One such classification is to determine how a cost behaves as the production level changes. For a fixed cost, the total amount does not change as the business's level of output varies. For a variable cost, the total amount *does* change as output varies. Once a business has determined which costs are fixed and which are variable, it can engage in cost-volume profit analysis. Such analysis lets a business know how many units it must sell in order to break even or to earn a profit of a given size. Conversely, the business can calculate how much profit it will earn if it produces and sells a given amount of units.

Another useful way to categorize costs is as either product costs or period costs. Product costs are all the costs that a business incurs to produce or purchase the goods or services that it sells. Product costs first appear as an asset (Inventory) on the balance sheet and eventually show up as Cost of Goods Sold on the income statement.

Period costs are all costs that are not product costs. They are usually related to selling or administrative functions. Period costs are recorded as expenses in the period in which they are incurred.

In order to make good decisions, a business must know how much it costs to perform various activities (i.e., produce a given product or operate a given department). A cost object is any such thing (product, department, etc.) for which we would like a cost measurement.

Direct costs are costs that can be directly traced to a specific cost object. Direct product costs include direct materials and direct labor. Indirect costs are costs that cannot be directly traced to specific cost objects. Indirect product costs are also referred to as manufacturing overhead. Indirect product costs are categorized as indirect materials, indirect labor, or other manufacturing overhead. Because indirect costs cannot be directly *traced* to specific cost objects, they must be *allocated* to cost objects.

Cost assignment is the process of assigning costs to cost objects. Cost assignment consists of *tracing* direct costs to cost objects and *allocating* indirect costs to cost objects.

Activity-based costing is a system for allocating indirect costs. The line of thinking behind activity-based costing is that there are certain activities ("cost drivers") that drive up overhead costs. If a product requires a lot of those cost-driving activities, more overhead should be allocated to that product.

Job order costing is a method of cost assignment that is used when a business makes unique, made-to-order products. In job order costing, each job is a cost object. That is, we want to track costs by job. As a result, each job has its own Work-in-Process subaccount.

Process costing is a method of cost assignment that is used when a business makes a very large quantity of identical units of a product. In process costing, costs are tracked by department (i.e., each department gets a Work-in-Process subaccount), then allocated to units.

Budgeting is an important part of cost accounting and managerial accounting. A major goal of the budgeting process is to avoid encountering surprise shortfalls. For example, how many units of inventory will we need to produce in order to have enough on hand to satisfy sales? How many units of raw materials will we have to purchase in order to produce the required number of units? Will we have enough cash to satisfy our expenses and other liabilities, or do we have to plan to cut costs or raise cash in some other way (e.g., borrowing)?

The budgeting process starts with the sales budget, then works backwards from there to determine the activities and expenses that will be necessary to satisfy the budgeted level of sales. The budgeting process often requires multiple iterations in order to develop a workable plan.

Variance analysis (i.e., comparing actual results to budgeted amounts) is the natural follow-up to the budgeting process. It provides information for preparing a more accurate budget for the following period. And it helps identify potential problems. Large variances, whether favorable or unfavorable, merit investigation so that the business can determine a) the cause of the variance and b) whether or not action is required to address the cause of the variance.

Appendix

A Very Brief Review of Accounting Basics

What follows is an extremely brief review of the most basic accounting concepts, in case you need to brush up.

The Accounting Equation

The most fundamental thing to know in accounting is the "accounting equation," which states that at all times and without exception:

Assets = Liabilities + Owner's Equity

"Assets" refers to everything that the business owns. Liabilities are all of the amounts the business owes to other parties. And owner's equity is essentially the amount "left over." (By way of analogy, if you own a $300,000 home and have a $100,000 mortgage, you have a $300,000 asset, a $100,000 liability, and $200,000 of equity.)

Financial Statements

There are four primary financial statements that businesses prepare: the balance sheet, the income statement, the statement of cash flows, and the statement of retained earnings.

The balance sheet shows the assets, liabilities, and owner's equity of the business at a particular moment in time. In other words, it's a depiction of the business's current condition with respect to the accounting equation.

The income statement shows the business's revenues and expenses over the period in question. A commonly used analogy is that if the balance sheet is a photograph, showing the business at one moment in time, then the income statement is a movie, showing the business over a period of time.

The cash flow statement shows all of the business's cash inflows and outflows during the period. This is different from the income statement, because the income statement works on an accrual basis rather than a cash basis. That is, the income statement reflects revenue when it is earned and expenses when they are incurred—regardless of when the cash actually changes hands. Also, the cash flow statement shows cash flows that are neither revenue nor expenses (e.g., cash inflow from issuing new shares or debt, or cash outflow from purchasing a new asset).

The statement of retained earnings details the changes in a company's retained earnings over the period. Retained earnings refers to the sum of all of the company's undistributed profits over the entire existence of the company. We say "undistributed" in order to distinguish from profits that have been distributed to company shareholders in the form of dividend payments.

Journal Entries: Debits and Credits

Every time a business engages in a transaction, a journal entry is made to record the event. Debits and credits are the terms used for the two halves of each journal entry.

For example, the following entry would be made if a business took on a $40,000 liability (a note payable) in order to purchase equipment:

DR. Equipment   40,000
     CR. Notes Payable   40,000

In each journal entry, the account that is debited is listed first, and the account that is credited is listed second, with an indentation to the right. Also, debit is conventionally abbreviated as "DR" and credit is abbreviated as "CR." (Often, these abbreviations are omitted, and credits are signified solely by the fact that they are indented.)

    An easy way to keep everything straight is to think of "debit" as meaning "left," and "credit" as meaning "right." That is, debits appear on the left-hand side of a journal entry, and they increase accounts on the left side of the accounting equation (i.e., assets). Credits appear on the right-hand side of a journal entry, and they increase accounts on the right side of the accounting equation (i.e., liabilities and owner's equity).

Reducing the balance in an account requires an entry of the opposite kind. That is, because asset accounts are increased by debits, they are decreased by credits. And liability and owner's equity accounts are increased by credits, so they are decreased by debits.

For example, the following journal entry would be made if a business uses cash to pay off a $10,000 balance owed to a vendor (i.e., an account payable):

Accounts Payable	10,000	
Cash		10,000

Accounts Payable is a liability, so we decrease it with a debit. And cash is an asset, so we decrease it with a credit.

Revenue accounts work like owner's equity accounts (i.e., they are increased by credits and decreased by debits), because they ultimately increase owner's equity. And expense accounts work in the opposite way of owner's equity accounts (i.e., they are increased by debits and decreased by credits), because they decrease owner's equity.

For example, the following entry would be made if a business is paid in cash for $10,000 worth of consulting services:

Cash	10,000	
Consulting Revenue		10,000

Cash is an asset account, so we increase it with a debit. And Consulting Revenue is a revenue account, so we increase it with a credit.

And the following entry would be made to record rent expense for a given month:

Rent Expense	6,000	
Rent Payable		6,000

Rent Expense is an expense account, so we increase it with a debit. And Rent Payable is a liability account, so we increase it with a credit. (Alternatively, if the rent were actually paid at the time the entry was recorded, the credit would have been to Cash instead of Rent Payable.)

Acknowledgements

As always, a heartfelt "thank you" goes to my editing team: Debbi, Pat, and Kalinda. And special thanks goes to Dan Kelly for sharing his time and expertise as technical editor.

About the Author:

Mike is the author of several financial books as well as the popular blog ObliviousInvestor.com. He is a Missouri licensed CPA. Mike's writing has been featured in many places, including *The Wall Street Journal*, *Money*, *Forbes*, *MarketWatch*, and Morningstar.

Also by Mike Piper:

Accounting Made Simple: Accounting Explained in 100 Pages or Less

Microeconomics Made Simple: Basic Microeconomic Principles Explained in 100 Pages or Less

Taxes Made Simple: Income Taxes Explained in 100 Pages or Less

Investing Made Simple: Investing in Index Funds Explained in 100 Pages or Less

Independent Contractor, Sole Proprietor, and LLC Taxes Explained in 100 Pages or Less

LLC vs. S-Corp vs. C-Corp Explained in 100 Pages or Less

Can I Retire? Managing Your Retirement Savings Explained in 100 Pages or Less

Social Security Made Simple: Social Security Retirement Benefits and Related Planning Topics Explained in 100 Pages or Less

INDEX

CPSIA information can be obtained
at www.ICGtesting.com
Printed in the USA
LVHW111536170920
666357LV00001B/152

9 780997 946529